White Fragility in Chimamanda Ngozi Adichie's Contemporary Novel "Americanah"

GRIN☺

Bibliographic information published by the German National Library:

The German National Library lists this publication in the National Bibliography; detailed bibliographic data are available on the Internet at http://dnb.dnb.de.

ISBN: 9783389024546
This book is also available as an ebook.

© GRIN Publishing GmbH
Trappentreustraße 1
80339 München

Print and binding: Books on Demand GmbH, Norderstedt, Germany
Printed on acid-free paper from responsible sources.

The present work has been carefully prepared. Nevertheless, authors and publishers do not incur liability for the correctness of information, notes, links and advice as well as any printing errors.

GRIN web shop: https://www.grin.com/document/1474080

Department of English and American Studies

Winter Term 2020/21

Being Black in America

White Fragility in Chimamanda Ngozi Adichie's Contemporary Novel *Americanah*

ZFBA Englischsprachige Literatur und Kultur
und Erziehungswissenschaften

1.Introduction

> "So you still blogging?" "Yes." "About race?" "No, just about life. Race doesn't really
> work here. I feel like I got off the plane in Lagos and stopped being black." (Adichie
> 475-476)

In this quote, Ifemelu, the black protagonist of Chimamanda Ngozi's novel *Americanah*
concludes that being black is no longer linked to discrimination and social disadvantages when
she returns from America to her home country Nigeria (Adichie 376). According to national
polling data, however, a majority of whites in America is oblivious to discrimination against
people of colour (Gallagher 23). Gallagher alarms that America has become a colour-blind
nation that does not recognise race based inequality (23). Whites seem to believe collectively
that people of colour have equal chances in employment, house ownership and in achieving
middle class status as whites (23). On top, the media constantly influences Americans with
biased representations of race relations that paint a picture of racial discriminating no longer
existing and being an issue of the past (23). Consequently, Americans seldomly experience
racial tension and discomfort, because they are insulated from racial stress (DiAngelo *White
Fragility* 6). However, up until today, black people in America live in a society that
systematically privileges white people and oppresses people of colour (DiAngelo "What is
Racism" 87). Several defensive reactions may follow when whites are confronted with their
privileged position in conversations about race (DiAngelo "White Fragility" 247). Robin
DiAngelo talks about *White Fragility* when whites cannot cope with the uncomfortability of
racial tension in conversations (247). Defensive behaviours function to restore the racial
equilibrium and help to maintain white privilege, as they do not allow alternative racial
perspectives and open dialogues (247). White Fragility is also reflected in contemporary
African literature. In her fictional novel *Americanah* (2013), the black author Chimamanda
Ngozi Adichie intertwines her personal race experience with whiteness and raises awareness of
what it means to be black in America (Chinenye 6). *Americanah* is not only a tale of romance,
but it equally confronts how institutional racism functions in American society.

This paper claims that the fictional novel *Americanah* by Adichie uncovers how White
Fragility operates in everyday-life encounters with conversations about racism in America,
thereby raising awareness for racism as functioning on an institutional level, rather than on an

individual level. To prove this thesis, the paper is structured as follows: The first chapter offers a theoretical overview and defines racism and gives DiAngelo's considerations to White Fragility. The analysis examines White Fragility operating within the novel, through characters and Ifemelu's lifestyle blog. Finally, the paper's findings will be summarized and an outlook on further research will be given.

2. Theory Chapter

2.1. Definition of Racism

Beamon defines race as a social construct invented and manipulated by society , rather than a biological category (123). Races are "invented social categories , but they are *socially real* and reenacted in the everyday life in encounters in all sorts of situations and spaces" (Bonilla-Silva 1360). Racism is a system that bases value on and structures opportunities on phenotype and the way people look (Jones 9). The sociologist Robin DiAngelo defines racism as "a form of oppression in which one racial group dominates others" (107). That means whites are the dominant group, while people of colour belong to the minorized group (107). Privileges, resources and power are unequally distributed between whites and people of colour (108). Racism "encompasses economic, political, social, and institutional actions and beliefs" (108) that perpetuate a system of advantages for whites and disadvantages for people of colour. DiAngelo points out that racism does not "move back and forth" (*White Fragility* 17) , but continuously benefits white people which is historically and traditionally anchored and normalized in ideology. Moreover, only whites hold the power to turn racial prejudice and discrimination into racism by their ability to "infuse their racial prejudice into the laws, policies, practices, and norms of society in a way that people of colour do not" (DiAngelo "What is Racism" 88) .

Racism does not only function on an individual or personal level in the form of overt "face-to-face hostile acts of a person toward a racial group" (Beamon 122). This paper highlights the institutionalised form of racism: Jones defines "institutionalized racism … as the structures, policies, practices, and norms resulting in differential access to the goods, services, and opportunities of society by "race" "(10). He further elaborates,

With regard to material conditions, examples include differential access to quality education, sound housing, gainful employment, appropriate medical facilities, and a

clean environment. With regard to access to power, examples include differential access to information (including one's own history), resources (including wealth and organizational infrastructure), and voice (including voting rights, representation in government, and control of the media. (Jones 10)

Most white Americans consider racism to be an individual prejudice against people of colour according to DiAngelo ("New Racism" 129). When white people talk about racism, the prevailing idea is that racists are immoral individuals who intentionally and deliberately want to hurt other people because of their race (129). But if that is their idea of a racist, they will never be able to admit complicity with racism to themselves as that would label them as a bad person (DiAngelo "White Fragility" 248). They also believe social inequality is a result of individual failure, class or culture, and do not see a connection to racism (Gallagher 26). Moreover, Di Angelo claims that many whites believe racism to be an issue of the past that is no longer existent (DiAngelo *White Fragility* 17). Colour-blindness is a belief system that adheres to the idea that individuals are not judged and seen by their skin colour (Gallagher 26). It allows white Americans to consider themselves as politically progressive and racially tolerant (26). However, this also means that "color-blindness allows whites to be blind to or ignore the fact that racial and ethnic minorities lag behind whites on almost every quality of life measure" (26). Besides, Gallagher concludes that "Colorblindness allows whites to think about contemporary race relations as a clean slate where the crimes of slavery, Jim Crow, institutional racism and white privilege have been ended and the racist sins of their grandparents have been erased" (32-33).

2.2. White Fragility

Mandatory cultural competency courses are often the only incident in which whites are directly confronted with white dominance and white privilege (DiAngelo "White Fragility" 247). Even there, coded language obscures white privilege and racist images and perspectives are continually reproduced (247). Hence, most whites "are largely insulated from race-based stress, and consequently, have not developed the ability or stamina to cope with racial stress" (Ng et al. 4). When whites are confronted with discussions about racism, their internalised ideologies such as individualism, meritocracy or colour-blindness lead to intense emotional reactions and a range of defensive responses may follow (DiAngelo "White Fragility" 245). Consequently, whites become fragile in conversations about racism (DiAngelo *White Fragility* 6) Robin DiAngelo calls this phenomenon White Fragility and defines it as follows:

> *White fragility* is a state in which even a minimum amount of racial stress becomes intolerable, triggering a range of defensive moves. These moves include the outward display of emotions such as anger, fear, and guilt, and behaviors such as argumentation, silence, and leaving the stress- inducing situation. These behaviors, in turn, function to reinstate white racial equilibrium." ("White Fragility" 247)

Racial stress happens when whites' racial worldview is challenged (Di Angelo "White Fragility" 247). They experience the challenge and confrontation as both unfamiliar and uncomfortable (247). The interruption of what is racially familiar can appear in various forms (247). Challenges that trigger racial stress include people of colour sharing their experiences with racism without being considerate of whites' racial comfort, a white person pointing out white privilege and not showing solidarity with a racial worldview that denies white privilege, or receiving feedback on racist behaviour (247). White people get offended once their racial biases and assumptions are challenged by alternative experiences of black people (Di Angelo *White Fragility* 6).

When this happens, whites fall back on behaviours such as "withdrawal, defensiveness, crying, arguing, minimizing, ignoring" (247) to restore racial equilibrium. Whites frequently employ the tactic of self-defence, thereby positioning themselves as victimized, attacked and blamed (249). In so doing, they portray themselves as morally superior and deny their privilege of whiteness (249). They blame people of colour for their discomfort or mistreatment and reverse the challenge by claiming it is they who are unfairly treated, not people of colour (249). However, DiAngelo asserts that these responses seldomly happen consciously, but happen unconsciously without realising ("White Fragility" 248).

Robin DiAngelo concludes that the lack of stamina ultimately perpetuates white dominance, as whites cannot tolerate the mere suggestion of having white privilege, nor can they constructively engage with different racial worldviews ("White Fragility" 250). This means that white perspectives are continuously seen as universal (250). White Fragility secures white racial dominance as the strategies outdo those of people of colour because whites hold "the social, economic and cultural capital" and blacks people do not (248). That means, whites always have the upper hand in conversations about race. "White Fragility works to punish the person giving feedback and essentially bully them back into silence. It also maintains white solidarity- the tacit agreement that we will protect white privilege and not hold each other accountable for our racism." (252). Whites seem to minimise the experiences of blacks and punish them for challenging their racial worldview (252). That is why White Fragility is a powerful way to relegate people of colour to their place and keep whites in their position of power in society (252).

3. Analysis of *White Fragility* in *Americanah*

3.1. Plot Summary

The Nigerian protagonist Ifemelu immigrates to the United States to attend University there (Adichie 134). Gradually, she adjusts to being a black immigrant and learns what it means to be black in America: There, Ifemelu's blackness starts to have meaning and she encounters racism in numerous everyday life situations such as at the hair salon, within her relationship with Curt, a middle-class white, and also at her workplace (190). Because of her experiences with racism, she starts a lifestyle blog to raise awareness of institutionalised racism in America (McCoy 283). Her blog gains a wide audience and offers her a lucrative career (283). Finally, however, Ifemelu returns to Nigeria where she finds that being black does not carry political meaning (Adichie 475-476).

3.2. White Fragility in conversations with Curt and Laura

The novel's protagonist Ifemelu observes that White Fragility operates in conversations in which white racial worldviews are being challenged. In *Americanah*, Adichie crafts privileged white middle-class characters that become fragile in conversations about racism (McCoy 284). The author especially does this through the white characters Curt and Laura (284).

In America, Ifemelu starts a relationship with a white middle-class man (Adichie 294). Ifemelu begins to recognise the intricacies of *White Fragility* in encounters with her boyfriend Curt. When Ifemelu and Curt have a discussion on black women in lifestyle magazines, White Fragility can be identified in his response (Adichie 294). Curt picks up a copy of Ifemelu's lifestyle magazine and comments on it as follows (294). "This magazine's kind of racially skewed," he said. "What?" "Come on. Only black women featured?" "You're serious," she said. He looked puzzled. "Yeah." (Adichie 294) Curt is oblivious to the overrepresentation of white women in lifestyle magazines (McCoy 284). The representation of black women in the entire magazine makes Curt feel confused and bewildered since he is familiar with white presentations as the norm in society (284) . People of colour, however, are used to being highly underrepresented in fashion magazines and do not hold the social power to contest this (DiAngelo "What is Racism" 2012 88). Ifemelu wants to demonstrate to Curt why magazines like *Essence* exist and escorts him to a local bookstore (Adichie 295) . There, she challenges Curt to count how many black women are represented in fashion magazines (295). Curt reluctantly admits that only three black women are depicted in all fashion magazines available at the local bookstore (295). Ifemelu lectures him on the consequences of magazines that predominantly feature white women as universal (295). She explains that she cannot find inspiration or value in the magazines as a black woman because make-up and fashion tips only apply to a white female audience with fair skin (295). The white perspective is anchored and solidified as the norm (DiAngelo "What is Racism" 2012 88). Ifemelu challenges Curt's racial worldview without being considerate of his white racial comfort (Adichie 295). This confrontation with his racism makes him feel uncomfortable and he becomes fragile and responds as follows," "Okay, babe, okay. I didn't mean for it to be such a big deal," he said." (295). While Curt does not respond with anger, fear or guilt, the discomfort of enduring a confrontation with racism makes him resort back to minimising his previous remark and thereby being able to withdraw from the stress-inducing situation (Di Angelo "White Fragility" 247). His response shows that he does not have enough stamina to reflect on alternative racial perspectives (those that Ifemelu explains to him) and endure the racial stress (247). Rather, Curt withdraws from the situation which ultimately secures white dominance as Ifemelu does not succeed in making an impact on broadening his racial worldview (DiAngelo "White Fragility" 252). Ifemelu is incredulous "towards Curt's inability to "get it " (McCoy 284) and contacts her friend Wambui in Nigeria and shares her experience – "the implicit biases, microaggressions, and everyday acts of institution-alized white racism that negate the existence of black people" (Mc Coy 284).

Not only does Ifemelu encounter White Fragility in her boyfriend's reactions, but she also experiences defensive responses when she confronts a white woman at her workplace (Adichie 168). Ifemelu works as a nanny for a white privileged family (Adichie 160). There she encounters White Fragility when she confronts Laura, her employer's sister, with her lack of historical knowledge about people of colour (168). The conversation starts when Laura points out that she met a new Nigerian doctor at a local practice (168).

> I read on the Internet that Nigerians are the most educated immigrant group in this country. Of course, it says nothing about the millions who live on less than a dollar a day back in your country, but when I met the doctor I thought of that article and of you and other privileged Africans who are here in this country. (Adichie 168)

Laura's remark reveals that she is colour-blind to racism and does not recognize her white privilege (Gallagher 26). Nor does she understand that racism operates on an institutional level and continuously disadvantages people of colour in America (26). She portrays herself as not being racist and labels Ifemelu as privileged to be able to work in America (Adichie 168). Colour-blindness enables Laura to regard racism as a thing of the past, which impact no longer carries meaning (Gallagher 33). Laura then continues the conversation by comparing the attitudes of an African woman she met in graduate school to that of an African American woman (Adichie 168). "She was wonderful, and she didn't get along with the African American woman in our class at all. She didn't have all those issues" (168). Ifemelu responds,

> Maybe when the African American's father was not allowed to vote because he was black, the Ugandan's father was running for parliament or studying at Oxford", Ifemelu said. Laura stared at her, made a mocking confused face. "Wait, did I miss something?" "I just think it's a simplistic comparison to make. You need to understand a bit more history," Ifemelu said. (…) "Well, I'll get my daughter and then go find some history books from the library, if I can figure out what they look like!" Laura said, and marched out. (Adichie 168)

This excerpt shows Laura's lack of racial stamina when she is confronted with race (Adichie 168). When Ifemelu points out that her comparison between a privileged African and a black

American is simplistic, Laura reacts with anger (168). Her question, "Wait, did I miss something?" (168) demonstrates her confusion and bewilderment as she is not used to being confronted with history and its ongoing effects on African Americans (DiAngelo "White Fragility" 247). According to McCoy, "The history to which Ifemelu refers is the history of Jim Crow laws in the US and white supremacy's impediment of African Americans to achieve a prosperous livelihood due to a racial caste system … ; these legacies have ensured the enshrinement and institutionalization of racial hierarchies in the US" (290). Laura understands racism as an issue of the past and does not understand why and that it still carries meaning (Gallagher 26). Besides, Laura situates racism on the individual level and feels attacked in her self- concept of being a good, moral and racially tolerant person (DiAngelo "New Racism" 129). Her furious exclaim, "Well, I'll get my daughter and then go find some history books from the library, if I can figure out what they look like!" (Adichie 168) is sarcastic and underlines how she refuses to acknowledge racism and her complicity with it (Gallagher 32). Ultimately, she marches off to leave the uncomfortable confrontation (Adichie 168). Ng et al. point out that "Whites generally have low awareness of their own privilege, and any discussion on the topic will cause them to experience discomfort and stress" (4). Ifemelu's challenge did not have an impact on Laura's racial worldview since she offendedly withdrew from the conversation, rather than opening up to a dialogue in which differing racial interpretations and further questions are accepted and taken seriously (Adichie 168) . Hence, her defensive reaction restores the racial status by refusing to acknowledge any complicity with racism (DiAngelo "White Fragility" 252).

3.3. *White Fragility* and Ifemelu's blog

Apart from using white characters that are oblivious to their privileged position in society, Adichie employs Ifemelu's blog "Raceteenth: Various Observations about American Blacks (Those formerly known as Negroes) by a Non-American Black" (Mc Coy 281) as a medium to pick up the central theme of White Fragility. In her blog, Ifemelu shares her understanding of America's racial politics (281).

In her blog post "Friendly Tips for the American Non-Black: How to React to an American Black Talking about Blackness" (Adichie 325), Ifemelu provides the white readership with suggestions on how to respond to conversations on racism differently. She points out that whites should not respond to Black Americans by arguing that class or gender are valid reasons for their racial experiences instead, and thereby denying racism (325). Minimising the experiences of racial discrimination is a common form of White Fragility in conversations about race (Di Angelo "White Fragility" (247). Moreover, she writes "Don't say "Oh, racism is over, slavery was so long ago." (Adichie 326) which is a form of trying to withdraw from having to acknowledge white privilege. By claiming that racism does not exist anymore, whites deny institutional racism and white privilege (Gallagher 33).

> Finally, don't put on a Let's Be Fair tone and say "But black people are racist too." Because of course, we're all prejudiced (I can't even stand some of my blood relatives, grasping, selfish folks), but racism is about the power of a group and in America it's white folks who have that power. How? Well, white folks don't get treated like shit in upper-class African American communities and white folks don't get denied bank loans or mortgages precisely because they are white and black juries don't give white criminals worse sentences than black criminals for the same crime and black police officers don't stop white folk for driving while white and black companies don't choose not to hire somebody because their name sounds white and black teachers don't tell white kids that they're not smart enough to be doctors and black politicians don't try some tricks to reduce the voting power of white folks through gerrymandering and advertising agencies don't say they can't use white models to advertise glamorous products because they are not considered "aspirational" by the "mainstream." (317)

This excerpt tackles the common white response of arguing that black people are racist too (DiAngelo "White Fragility" 247). Ifemelu explains that prejudice adheres to a definition of individual racism, while racism is actually institutionalised in a system of white dominance (327). She highlights that only whites hold the power to turn racial prejudice into racism (Adichie 317).

The blogpost "To My Fellow Non-American Blacks: In America, You Are Black, Baby" (Adichie 220) shows the strategy of white self-defensiveness in racial confrontations. Ifemelu explains to other Non-American blacks what happens when they voice anger about racism (221).

> If you're telling a non-black person about something racist that happened to you, make sure you are not bitter. Don't complain. Be forgiving. If possible, make it funny. Most

of all, do not be angry. Black people are not supposed to be angry about racism. Other-
wise you get no sympathy. This applies only for white liberals, by the way. Don't even
bother telling a white conservative about anything racist that happened to you. Because
the conservative will tell you that YOU are the real racist and your mouth will hang
open in confusion. (221)

Here, Ifemelu warns her readership about White Fragility when challenging whites' racial
worldview and sharing racist experiences with them, especially with white conservatives
(Adichie 221). Claiming that blacks are the real racists is a form of self-defensiveness and happens when whites feel attacked and blamed (DiAngelo "White Fragility" 249). Whites deny
their privileged position and reverse the challenge, so that blacks are bullied back into silence
(DiAngelo "White Fragility" 252). People of colour stop sharing their experiences with racism
because they fear being attacked for it (252). Moreover, Ifemelu hints at whites' racial comfort
when she writes "Most of all, do not be angry. Black people are not supposed to be angry"
(Adichie 221). Ifemelu understands that whites lack racial stamina to respond to racial confrontations adequately (221).

As her blog gained popularity, corporations ask Ifemelu to give presentations and hold diversity workshops about racism in America (Adichie 304).

Her presentation was titled "How to talk about race with colleagues of other races", but
who, she wondered, would they be talking to, since they were all white? Perhaps the
janitor was black That evening she received an e-mail: YOUR TALK WAS BALO-
NEY. YOU ARE A RACIST. YOU SHOULD BE GRATEFUL WE LET YOU INTO
THIS COUNTRY.That e-mail, written in all capital letters, was a revelation. The point
of diversity workshops, or multicultural talks, was not to inspire any real change but to
leave people feeling good about themselves. (Adichie 304-305)

In this incident, White Fragility comes in the form of self-defensiveness and outrage
(Adichie 304-305). A white person feels offended by her lecture and denies their privileged
position in society (DiAngelo *White Fragility* 6). Moreover, the white person situates racism
on the individual level. "You should be grateful we let you into this country" (Adichie 305).
That means that the writer does not acknowledge the power whites hold on an institutional level
above people of colour , but feels personally offended by the mere suggestion that racism
against people of colour exists (DiAngelo *White Fragility* 6). They do not want to be labelled

as being racist, as that would make them an immoral person on the individual level (DiAngelo "New Racism" 129). Moreover, Ifemelu realises that a direct confrontation with racism is not even possible in diversity workshops (Adichie 305). Even there, white privilege needs to be obscured to maintain whites' racial comfort (DiAngelo "White Fragility" 247). Consequently, Ifemelu is "bullied back into silence" (252) and in the subsequent diversity workshops, she adjusts her approach to make white people feel good and moral about themselves (Adichie 305).

4. Conclusion

Firstly, it was noted that race is not defined as a biological category, but as a social construct that impacts all areas of life. To define racism, this paper draws on DiAngelo's theoretical considerations that racism is a form of oppression in which whites dominate people of colour in terms of privileges, resources, and power in society. Further, racial prejudice and discrimination can only be used by whites to be infused into laws and norms since black people do not hold the social power to do so. Moreover, institutional racism is explained as the different access to services, opportunities, and power between whites and people of colour based on race. That means, that quality education, employment, and also representation in government or the access to controlling what is represented in the media is unequally distributed to the advantage of whites. Di Angelo asserts that most Americans believe that racism is a moral issue linked to individual hostile acts against people of colour. They see themselves as politically progressive and racially tolerant because they adopt a colour-blind perspective from which they do not judge people on their race. However, colour-blindness makes whites oblivious to their inherited white privilege and makes it impossible for them to recognize institutionalized racism. Since whites are seldomly aware of their own racial privilege, they experience discomfort and stress when they are confronted with racism in conversations with fellow whites or people of colour. Their insulation from confrontations with racism explains why whites cannot cope constructively in conversations and respond defensively and offendedly. DiAngelo calls this phenomenon White Fragility. DiAngelo asserts that white fragility perpetuates white dominance as whites cannot acknowledge or recognize their privileged position in society. The obliviousness to white privilege hinders whites from a constructive dialogue in which black perspectives, experiences and opinions are heard and validated. White Fragility helps to silence black voices on racism and secures white perspectives as universal.

It can be detected that the thesis statement is valid. Adichie uncovers how White Fragility operates in everyday-life encounters with racism in America, thereby leading the American reader to understand racism as functioning on an institutional level, rather than on an individual level. Adichie takes the reader through numerous encounters, in which whites become highly fragile in confrontations with racism. She does this through white characters and also tackles White Fragility in Ifemelu's lifestyle blog and diversity workshops. The protagonist Ifemelu , who is a Nigerian immigrant in America begins to understand how racism functions on an institutional level. Ifemelu experiences White Fragility in conversations with her white boyfriend Curt and her employer's sister Laura but also in responses to her lifestyle blog where she thematizes racism , as well as in diversity workshops that she holds. In these encounters, whites are oblivious to their inherited white privilege and react defensively once Ifemelu confronts them with their racist impact. Possible avenues for further research would be examining another contemporary novel that deals with racism to compare how racism is defined.

Works Cited List

Adichie, Chimamanda Ngozi. *Americanah*. 4th Estate, 2017.

Beamon, Krystal. "Racism and Stereotyping on Campus: Experiences of African American Male Student-Athletes." *The Journal of Negro Education*, vol. 83, no. 2, 2014, pp. 121–134.

Bonilla-Silva, Eduardo. "The Structure of Racism in Color-Blind, 'Post-Racial' America." *American Behavioral Scientist*, vol. 59, no. 11, 2015, pp. 1358–1376.

DiAngelo, Robin. "WHITE FRAGILITY." *Counterpoints*, vol. 497, 2016, pp. 245–253.

DiAngelo, Robin. "What is Racism." *Counterpoints*, vol. 497, 2016, pp.107-124.

DiAngelo, Robin. "Chapter 7: What Is Racism?" *Counterpoints*, vol. 398, 2012, pp. 87–103.

DiAngelo, Robin. "New Racism." *Counterpoints*, vol. 497, 2016, pp.107-124.

DiAngelo, Robin. *White Fragility: Why It's so Hard for White People to Talk about Racism*. Beacon Press, 2020.

Gallagher, Charles A. "Color-Blind Privilege: The Social and Political Functions of Erasing the Color Line in Post Race America." *Race, Gender & Class*, vol. 10, no. 4, 2003, pp. 22–37.

Jones, Camara Phyllis. "Confronting Institutionalized Racism." *Phylon (1960-)*, vol. 50, no. 1/2, 2002, pp. 7–22

Ng, Eddy S., et al. "White and Minority Employee Reactions to Perceived Discrimination at Work: Evidence of White Fragility?" International Journal of Manpower, ahead-of-print, no. ahead-of-print, 2020.

YOUR KNOWLEDGE HAS VALUE

- We will publish your bachelor's and
  master's thesis, essays and papers

- Your own eBook and book -
  sold worldwide in all relevant shops

- Earn money with each sale

Upload your text at www.GRIN.com
and publish for free